BLEAK MUSIC

POEMS & PHOTOGRAPHS
of the American Southwest

Jeffrey C. Alfier, Photographer

Larry D. Thomas, Poet

BLUE HORSE PRESS REDONDO BEACH, CALIFORNIA   2016

BLEAK MUSIC

POEMS & PHOTOGRAPHS
of the American Southwest

Jeffrey C. Alfier, Photographer

Larry D. Thomas, Poet

Blue Horse Press
P.O. Box 7000 - 760
Redondo Beach,
California 90277

Copyright © 2016 by Jeffrey C. Alfier
and Larry D. Thomas
All rights reserved.
Printed in the United States of America.

Cover art: *Cutbank Beyond Twentynine Palms*
by J.C. Alfier

Editors: Jeffrey and Tobi Alfier
Blue Horse Press logo: Amy Lynn Hayes

ISBN 978-0692718919

These poems are for Jeffrey C. Alfier, whose photographs and poems I have long admired.

Larry D. Thomas

Table of Contents

I. No Roof but Sky

Photo: Joshua Tree	1
Joshua Trees	2
Photo: Furnace Creek Wash, Death Valley	3
Furnace Creek Wash	4
Photo: Desert Center, California	5
Out Here	6
Photo: Horses on the Mexican Border	7
Horses on the Mexican Border	8
Photo: Mesquite Sentinel	9
Mesquite Sentinel	10
Photo: Vanishing River	11
Vanishing River	12
Photo: Somewhere Between Marfa and Lobo	13
"LIMOUSIN BULLS"	14
Photo: Just Outside of Alpine	15
Just Outside Alpine	16
Photo: Pecos River Barn Swallows	17
Barn Swallows	18

II. Phantom Footfall

Photo: Death Valley Borax Works	21
Death Valley Borax Works	22
Photo: Rhyolite	23
Blue Shadow	24
Photo: Death Valley Junction	25
Violent Business	26
Photo: Barstow Railyard	27

Barstow Railyard	28
Photo: Beatty, Nevada	29
Poor Church in Beatty, Nevada	30
Photo: Trucks Near Naco	31
Trucks	32
Photo: Nightfall in Benson	33
Reb's Café	34
Photo: Lobo, Texas	35
Lobo, Texas	36
Photo: Leaving Lobo	37
An Imposing Quadrilateral	38
Photo: Valentine Café	39
"Hi Way Café"	40
Photo: Coyanosa, South of FM 1450	41
Deserted School Bus	42
Author Bios	

ACKNOWLEDGMENTS

San Pedro River Review   Death Valley Borax Works

*When words become unclear, I shall focus with photographs.
When images become inadequate,
I shall be content with silence.*

Ansel Adams

I. No Roof but Sky

The question is from where one sees the sky.

Odysseus Elytis

Joshua Tree

Joshua Trees
(Joshua Tree National Park, California)

Here, in the Mojave,
even the rare rain
is violent, pummeling
their supplicating visages
with the wrath of God.

The Mormons saw
their outstretched limbs
as the arms of Joshua
raised toward the heavens
in hard, hard prayer.

Some of their kind
endure a thousand years,
brooking the scourges
of drought and savage
windblast, keeping

their locked-open eyes
fixed on the unforgiving
sun, each a weary Job
seeking but a trace
of grace or fickle mercy.

Furnace Creek Wash, Death Valley

Furnace Creek Wash
(Death Valley, California)

The arid features
of a mountain
cast shadows

black as crude oil.
A narrow stream
chisels its futile passage

through rock
and blistering gravel,
slithering toward

a sizzling death
of steam. What relief
exists looms high above

in the cloudless cerulean
sky: the putative relief
of the vacuum.

Desert Center, California

Out Here
(Desert Center, California)

The diamond-shaped sign
reading "END" is redundant,
given the vast desertscape

stretching for miles behind it
to mountains choked blue
with desiccation. Green

is dark, uninviting, pulsing
in a solitary creosote bush
indulging its greed for moisture.

In shadow, "END" flaunts
its fatuous presence, absurd
out here as "GENESIS."

Horses on the Mexican Border

Horses on the Mexican Border
(Arizona)

Some seem to be
grazing the grassless
surface of the dirt road.
They wander oblivious

of the hardscrabble hills
rising behind them,
their broad backs
concave with the weight

of phantom saddles.
Blessed with the nuanced
wisdom of horse sense,
they could care less

who will mount them next,
whether deputy sheriff
or Pancho Villa, as long
as the rider is a maestro

of the arduous art
of horse-handling,
free of the repugnant
stench of fear.

Mesquite Sentinel

Mesquite Sentinel
(Saguaro National Park, Arizona)

Mizquitl, the Aztecs
named you. You were sacred
as the hearts of virgins,
throbbing in the hands

of priests as offerings
to the gods. Obdurate
in death as in the torturous
centuries of eking out life

in the desert, you cradle
Father Sky in brazen arms
gnarled for strength by the bloody,
obstetric hands of *Cihuacoatl* *.

The giant saguaros surround you,
standing erect in rapt attention,
eavesdropping the wind-whispered
subtlety of your lessons.

* Aztec goddess of childbirth and fertility

Vanishing River

Vanishing River
(Cochise County, Arizona)

The lost
who stagger to its edge
drop to their knees,
hallucinating the dream

of water.
Seasons back,
a monsoon rain
hacked its banks

with the red-brown blade
of an axe.
The sere wind
hardens the heart

of mesquite.
Above the lavender
mountains, clouds gather
like family at a deathbed.

Somewhere Between Marfa and Lobo

"LIMOUSIN BULLS"
(near Valentine, Texas)

Some say their breed
dates back to the drawings
in the French Lascaux Cave.

Their harsh environment
buttressed their hardiness.
With the ease of first light,

they masticated dry grass
into the mass of muscle.
It's no wonder the brash,

carmine letters of their name
brazen it out to this day
on the side of a barn

unused for decades:
the brash, carmine letters
tough as the creosote-

soaked railroad ties
jumbled by baby gods
for a game of pick-up sticks.

Just Outside of Alpine

Just Outside Alpine
(dead mule deer, far West Texas)

Its hide is ragged
as the garment
of a beggar.

Even the grasses
haloing it
lie prostrate

as if hammered
by the blacksmith
of the gods.

Its brain and tongue
are leather.
For weeks reduced

to the lowest
common denominator
of hide and bone,

its head's
still angled skyward.
Its parched mouth,

locked slightly open,
still groans its bleak,
unanswerable prayer.

Pecos River Barn Swallows

Barn Swallows
(Pecos River, far West Texas)

Startled beneath
the farm-to-market
highway bridge,

they blast like shrapnel
to safety in the arms
of Father Sky.

Plastered to concrete girders,
their nests are cups
of mud pellets

lined with feathers
and grass the texture of nylon.
Though they soar the heavens

like legions of iridescent
steel blue angels, their young,
earthbound for nurturing

with the regurgitated pabulum
of their parents,
stretch wide open their bright

yellow beaks, and,
like an offbeat, off-key quartet,
belt out their chirrups of survival.

II. Phantom Footfall

Let us go on, since the old road
will meet us on our way –
   It is sad, rugged, deserted. . .
though still the home of white phantoms
     we once adored.

    Rosalia de Castro, from *The River Sar*

Death Valley Borax Works

Death Valley Borax Works
(California)

The music of the iron
is Stravinsky
navigating the atonal
harmonies of rust;
the song of the adobe,
the centuries-long
diminuendo to dust.

Of this godforsaken plant,
but the iron
and adobe survive
where borax was purified
from a badlands lakebed
abundant with ore.
The ominous mountain

in the foreground,
surfaced with rocks
and pebbles, is sepia;
those in the backdrop,
soft with the blue
and lavender washes
of the otherworld.

One who listens
hard enough, turning
an ear to the searing,
perpetual breeze,
can hear the creaking,
sweat-frothed harnesses
of a thousand mules.

Rhyolite

Blue Shadow
(Death Valley, California)

Half of a three-
story building
sorrows
in the rubble
at its base.

A mountain
of rhyolite,
as one might see
in a moonscape,
creaks in sunlight.

Both the building
and the sun-
baked brush
of the desert,
engulfed

in blue
shadow,
shriek the bleak
music
of departure.

Death Valley Junction

Violent Business
(Death Valley, California)

Three water storage tanks,
forsaken; four telephone
poles, ages devoid
the staticky transmission
of a voice; and a desolate

mountain dominating
the backdrop, dramatizing
the foreground of dead,
whispering brush.
Rust envelops the tanks

like tightly-fitted gloves,
strangling the dream
of water.
The poles list
like Christ-less crosses,

their uprights truncated
at their transverses,
unfit even
for the crucifixion
of thieves.

The mountain
usurps the backdrop
like a bruised sheriff,
obsessed with his violent
business of light, shadow.

Barstow Railyard

Barstow Railyard
(Barstow, California)

Dozens of tracks,
naked for umpteen years
to the fire and ice

of desert days and nights,
languish in pitiless sun.
In shadow, the steel wheels

of a dirty, off-white railcar
gleam like polished silver.
Power poles, laid out

in straight lines
and stinking with creosote,
thrust pitch-dark hopes

into the sky.
Everything, the tracks,
wheels, railcars, poles, hopes,

and even the curved,
illusive relief
of nearby bone-dry mountains,

clickety-clacks,
hurtling toward the point
of vanishment.

Beatty, Nevada

Poor Church in Beatty, Nevada

A weathered, brown door
no larger than that of a house
opens right into the sanctuary.
The spire juts into the cloudless sky

as much as its modesty will allow.
The bléssed poor, in spirit
and in coins for Caesar, worship there.
On the same small lot of the church,

within feet of unstained-glass windows
smothered by a storage shed,
a massive billboard rises, dwarfing
the humble spire, soliciting patrons

for gambling, fast food, and cheap lodging.
Shadows, ubiquitous and cancerous
as sin, butt against the edge of the lot.
The Joshua tree is genuflecting.

Trucks Near Naco

Trucks
(near Naco, Arizona)

The headlights of her eyes,
still intact, stare right at me.
Her grill is the aftermath

of a slugfest, a mouth
hardly recognizable, savagely
reshaped by an attacker.

Long abandoned to the sun,
left to the skullduggery
of ruin, she contemplates

the dismantled remnants
of the truck beside her.
What's left of her skin

is flaky, friable, beyond
the redemption of lotion.
She stares straight ahead,

a catatonic hag in a wheelchair,
her iron face smug beneath
her caked makeup of rust.

Nightfall in Benson

Reb's Café
(Benson, Arizona)

Reb's Café,
in yellow neon,
is a desert David

psyched up for combat
against the indigo Goliath
of the sky.

A lone customer
meets the night
for coffee there,

bundled in his black
woolen topcoat.
The screened windows

shield him from the glare
of a passerby, buttressing
his cherished privacy.

Hopper's *Nighthawks**
envy him the purity
of his solitude.

*oil on canvas by Edward Hopper, 1942

Lobo, Texas

Lobo, Texas

The brush, grass,
yucca, and cacti
are wrecking it,
fragment by fragment,

this *station*
long relieved
of *service*.
The worthless cover

over the driveway
is a monument
to fade, peel, splinter,
and rust. *Lobo*

looms above
the boarded up
plate glass window
like an apocalyptic

howl, piercing the icy,
discomfiting blue
of the sky.
Texas appears

on the building
in the backdrop
the only way it can:
at a distance.

Leaving Lobo

An Imposing Quadrilateral
(Lobo, far West Texas)

of native stones
rises from the desert
like a bizarre monolith

dedicated to the memory
of oblivion. A large
rectangular sign once inset

in the quadrilateral is gone.
The West Texas sky
now occupies the rectangle

like a canvas of deep blue
"Vacancy." What the sign
represented is anyone's

guess. But the stones
endure, the same stones
the desert's always owned,

just rearranged for a few
decades as if the desert
felt it'd try something new.

Valentine Café

"Hi Way Café"
(Valentine, far West Texas)

Its façade's a crumbling,
peach-colored intimation
of the Alamo.
Whoever made the door
never made doors

for a living.
His tool box
was makeshift, his tools
alien to the angles
of a square.

Bereft for years
of its last customer
who bought but a single
cup of coffee,
it stands a cracked shrine

to a desert hamlet
well into its death throes
the day a cheap sign
was flipped from "closed"
to "open." The locals

never noticed when it opened,
never fretted when it closed,
smug in their knowledge
that, in the desert,
like "life" and "death,"

"open" and "closed"
were always nothing
but random sides
of the same
silverless coin.

Coyanosa, South of FM 1450

Deserted School Bus
(Coyanosa, far West Texas)

Creosote bushes,
ornery as freckle-
faced, unkempt

schoolboys,
crowd around
its frozen-shut doors.

Its grueling,
hushed demise
belies the sky

studded with clouds
of stuffed animals.
It ebbs, a husk

of what it was,
its dust-caked seats
so tumid with longing

for the antics of kids
they've cracked
wide open.

Jeffrey C. Alfier is winner of the 2014 Kithara Book Prize, judged by Dennis Maloney. He has been nominated for eight Pushcarts, and is a two-time nominee for the UK's Forward Prize for Poetry. In 2013 he was selected as a finalist for the Press 53 Poetry Contest. Publication credits include *Copper Nickel, Crab Orchard Review, Iron Horse Literary Review, Kestrel, Hotel Amerika, Permafrost, Poetry Ireland Review, South Carolina Review, Southwestern American Literature, Spoon River Poetry Review,* and *Texas Review.* He is author of two collections of Southwest poems: *The Wolf Yearling,* and *Idyll for a Vanishing River.* He is also author of *The Storm Petrel, The Red Stag at Carrbridge,* and most recently, *Southbound Express to Bay Head — New Jersey Poems.*

Larry D. Thomas, a member of the Texas Institute of Letters, served as the 2008 Texas Poet Laureate. He has published several award-winning collections of poetry, and in numerous national journals. *As If Light Actually Matters: New & Selected Poems,* the most comprehensive and definitive collection of his poetry to date, was issued by *Texas Review* Press in 2015, and was selected as a *2015 Writers' League of Texas Book Awards Finalist.* Thomas will be the featured author for the 2017 Oswald Distinguished Writers Series (University of South Carolina, Aiken). His Web site address is www.larrydthomas.com.

www.ingramcontent.com/pod-product-compliance
Lightning Source LLC
Chambersburg PA
CBHW041528090426
42736CB00036B/232